earworms

Amyra Archuleta

BookLeaf Publishing

India | USA | UK

Presentation by *BookLeaf Publishing*

Web: www.bookleafpub.com

E-mail: info@bookleafpub.com

ISBN: 9789360943554

First edition 2024

One

Fade Into You - Mazzy Star

how to record life
when we were always moving
how to remember people
when I eventually had to say goodbye

when cities all seem different
and people's faces started to blur from memory

the songs
they stayed the same
they helped me remember

Two

Both Hands - Ani DiFranco

dancing in the living room
sometimes we would lose Sid
bearded dragons can be lost easily

I remember the night you came into my bed
naked and sobbing
hurt again by your boyfriend
I didn't know how to tell you that you deserved
so much better
or I tried and you couldn't hear me
We were so young then
love felt so big

Three

Southwest VooDoo - ICP

We drove out to the middle Rez
in a Honda Civic with giant speakers in the back
I thought it was a great idea
to drink a fifth of vodka mixed with Sunny D
it was not

woke up
backseat
passed out in Jeff's lap
he demanded I suck his dick
instead
I rolled down the window and threw up
get me the fuck out of this car
the stars were beautiful that night

I was so annoyed at everyone
my girlfriend's thought I was weird because I
wasn't obsessed with the smell of Raven's
hoodie
I thought they were weird because they were

I had to sing at Baccalaureate the next morning
in church

for the final in choir class
I mouthed the words
and hoped I didn't barf on the person in front of
me

Four

Motion Sickness - Phoebe Bridgers

Trying to act chill
you and guys sat down at the bar
having to bring you beer
and smiling
like
everything was okay

I was dying inside
could you see it
did you care

I should have believed her boyfriend
when he told me you were cheating
I believed you
said you loved me
asked me to get a job at the bar
was it so you could rub my face in it?
You told all of your friends that I was too cold
how was I supposed to
stay warm
when you treated me like I didn't matter

Five

I Love Living in the City - Fear

Middle of a hot Michigan Summer
I think I fell in love that day
in your car
on the way to get tacos

later in the dugout at the park
you showed me the Ninja Turtles
you had painted on the bench

it surprised me to see a version of you that
seemed happy
I wanted you to stay forever

Six

Your Best American Girl - Mitski

Portland always felt a little damp
and I always felt a little drunk
meeting my birth mom
was a trip I wasn't quite ready for

dirty apartment
methadone clinic
donuts and cocoa

I could have been more patient
I could have been less afraid

I tried my best mom
I tried my best

Seven

David Duchovny - Bree Sharp

do you remember when you were my best
friend?
high school happened
and everything changed
we used to talk on the phone
almost every night
about the latest episode of the X- Files
we were going to be FBI agents

Do you remember watching The Matrix six
times at the movie theater because nothing else
was playing

I think it started
that day at your dad's work party
we were wrestling
my shirt came up
I was wearing a bra
and you freaked out

friends started to ask if we were dating
we stopped talking

the truth is probably out there
somewhere

Eight

No Sleep Till Brooklyn - Beastie Boys

staying up all night on your porch
drinking wine and talking about everything
and nothing
I miss it
I miss you

Nine

Goodbye Horses - Q Lazarus

505 flophouse
acid trip band sessions in the basement
drinking games and broken hearts

we had a mantra
hood rat things
hood rat friends

we were so messy
it was almost beautiful

Ten

Superman - Goldfinger

it was the first time we were allowed to go to a
concert without our parents
it was the first time I saw a video about factory
farming
in the lobby
by the merch table

I tried to be vegan that Summer
but it was too hard to give up Hot Cheetos

it was the first time I felt hundreds of sweaty
bodies against mine
and it wasn't gross
and I didn't feel alone anymore

Eleven

...Baby One More Time

I know what it feels like to fall apart
I know what lonely feels like

when being hurt feels like love
and I would do anything for attention
affection

hit me baby one more time and
then tell me that you love me

Twelve

Who Writes Your Rules - Lower Class Brats

I'm sorry I look awkward in all the pictures
I didn't want to pose like a pin up

you were always trying to dress me up
you looked great
you always looked great

that was the difference between us
I didn't understand how to flirt yet
or why I would even want to

you wanted to date the boys in the band
and I wanted to be them

I tried so you wouldn't be so annoyed at me
I really did
but yep
still awkward

Thirteen

Blood Red Sentimental Blues - Cotton Jones

hey remember when we rode bikes around the
city?
Water bottles full of wine
Summer nights full of possibilities
nights of dancing only occasionally interrupted
by crying in the alley
there's something about summer nights in the
Midwest that feel infinite
like the warm will last forever
maybe you have to know what cold really feels
like in order to appreciate it

Fourteen

Talking to Myself - Prude Boys

Red headed cowboy drummer
marlboros, pbr, and depression
the band
seemed like the only thing that mattered to him
I canned peaches while he got drunk
I wanted to plant a garden
but I was too sad

Fifteen

Beat Your Heart Out - The Distillers

tallest man on earth
10 inch Mohawk
from another planet
Phoenix dessert heat
Record stores and bowling alleys
Brazilian goth vampire chica
the girl from Idaho
was wild
man
the Red Cross Safety Camp
was a good time

Sixteen

Nervous Breakdown - Black Flag

I thought strangers on the street were going to
start screaming at me
I couldn't leave my apartment
I couldn't text anyone back

Weeks of drifting in and out of sleep
sometimes feeling like I couldn't breathe
sporadic bouts of sobbing
didn't know what I was sad about

where do you go
when your thoughts turn on you

Seventeen

Wish You Were Here - Incubus

Do you remember
taking Exstacy and inventing slow moshing
Do you remember
my boyfriend leaving us at the concert
Do you remember
thinking we could walk home from Detroit
everything seemed possible

Eighteen

Between The Bars - Elliot Smith

I have never told you this but on that trip to
Cincinnati I kept looking for different ways to
kill myself
to create an elaborate escape plan
I kept quiet as you told me one of your favorite
stories again
I didn't want to feel that way but it was
unavoidable
My mind was attacking me and I didn't know
how to stop it

So I went to the bar with you guys and tried to
pretend that I was okay
that it was all okay

Nineteen

Talking Heads - This Must Be The Place

you're here
in my headphones
on the record player
on the radio
in the movie soundtracks

no matter how far away
or how long it has been since we last talked
even if we never talk again

anywhere there is music playing
you
are
still
here

www.ingramcontent.com/pod-product-compliance
Lightning Source LLC
LaVergne TN
LVHW050309200726
843509LV00015B/3247